Exit Lever

*How Smart Business Owners & Buyers Avoid
the 10 Mistakes that Ruin the Sales of
Businesses*

by Jeff Dousharm & Jethro Hopkins

Exit Lever
How Smart Business Owners & Buyers Avoid the 10 Mistakes that Ruin the Sales of Businesses

This Book Can Save You 6 Months and $135,000+

Copyright © 2018 No Coast Business Advisors

Jeff Dousharm
Jethro Hopkins

www.ExitLeverBook.com

All rights reserved.

Book cover and digital illustration by: **Brad Szollose**

Cover Photo Credit:
ShutterStock: ID: 529316230
Businessman walking towards his ambition

Printed in the United States of America
First Printing: October 2018

Published by: **Paradigm Impact**
Hello@ParadigmImpact.com

ISBN:
978-0-9977072-3-6

Disclaimer

Dedication

This book is dedicated to the business owners, entrepreneurs, professionals, and aspiring owners!

Our belief is that the values, work ethic, commitment, risk taking, and sacrifice that goes into being a business owner is overlooked by far too many people.

We know your struggle.

We've lived it.

We respect it.

We honor it.

Here is one of our favorite quotes and we believe it applies perfectly to business owners:

"The credit belongs to the person who is actually in the arena; whose face is marred by dust and sweat and blood; who strives valiantly; who errs and comes up short again and again; who knows the great enthusiasm, the devotion, and spends himself or herself in a worthy cause; who at best knows in the end the triumph of high achievement; and at worst, at least fails while daring greatly; so that his or her place shall never be with those cold and timid souls who know neither victory nor defeat."
~President Theodore Roosevelt

So whether you are a current, past, or future business owner - this book is dedicated to YOU!

Want access to additional FREE resources for buying or selling a business?

Simply go to:

www.ExitLeverBonus.com

Want more information on
No Coast Business Advisors?

Have more questions?

Then go to:

www.NoCoastBusinessAdvisors.com

Interested in becoming a
Business Broker yourself?

Check out:
www.NCBAbroker.com

***Be sure to flip to the final pages to also check out the Special Offers for Our Readers

Contents

Intro:
First Things First

Buying and selling businesses is a BIG deal.
And with it comes big problems and pitfalls.

Exit Lever is about protecting you during one of the most important transaction types of YOUR financial empire. We know that buying or selling businesses is a massive way to create, grow, and move wealth when it's done right. And when you follow the right steps, it can also <u>preserve</u> your time and money to put into the people and goals you care the most about in your life. That is what real success and freedom is all about.

Whether you are a centimillionaire acquiring a group of businesses and assets, or a solo-preneur selling off your first business that you've grown and scaled to now cash in on, the dangers are very similar and costly when you make mistakes. And for those who are serious - we are here to help.

So WHO should even bother turning the pages to read this book?

And WHY should you listen to us?

First off, WHO is this for?

**If you are planning to sell a business...
this book is for you!**

**If you are planning to buy a business...
this book is for you!**

AND

**If you want to get things right to increase the
value of your business...
this book is also for you!**

Because if you don't follow what we are going to share with
you, you may become another statistic that wastes 6 months
and $135,000+ by committing any of the avoidable mistakes
we are going to show you. And this lost time and money
can occur for both the Seller AND the Buyer!

These numbers are very conservative and not an attempt to
exaggerate for purposes of being overdramatic. There is
more than enough data to back these numbers, but let's
make it even easier rather than giving you pages of citations.

If you screw up a deal it can easily cost you 6+ months of
starting over the entire process for both Sellers and Buyers
in listing the business, offers, walk throughs, meetings,
financing, counter offers, closing etc. - that part is pretty
simple to consider the massive time loss.

But what about the money?

How could a little mistake or delay also result in over 6 figures of financial loss?

Here are a few basic numbers:
1. The average transaction for main street business sales is around $750,000.

2. Mistakes that results in re-listing a business, delays, and any issues that result in a modified sale price of the business ends up being a minimum average change of 18% (and not in the direction that favors you of course).

3. Just 18% of $750,000 is **$135,000!**

Now consider if the business is worth 1-2 million….the mistakes are even more costly whether you are the Buyer or the Seller!

So keep this in mind, and we'll remind you:

On average, 6 months and $135K+ are on the line with EVERY one of the issues we'll share….and the issues can compound and amplify!

And that's why we're here to help!

So WHY us?

Our names are Jeff Dousharm and Jethro Hopkins, and we own **No Coast Business Advisors**.

Though we own a Business Brokerage and love helping others buy and sell businesses, it wasn't always this way. We each started as business owners ourselves outside of this incredible profession long before building a Business Brokerage.

In fact, between us, we continue to operate multiple businesses and investments. This is part of why we are passionate about helping others do the same - we are just like you. We have marketed, negotiated, bought and sold millions of dollars worth of our own businesses, and have gone on to help with millions more of client transactions too.

So when we share behind the scenes information, it's not conjecture or theory. We've been there as the Buyer, as the Seller, and as the Business Broker. Just like you and many other business owners, we have fought the battles it takes to survive and grow businesses. We've been around the block more than a few times, earned the scars, and discovered the lessons that we now leverage in our own businesses and share with others.

We know each role and each view on how to maximize your position - **and what that means to you is that we can arm you with the tools and the skills you need to WIN!**

About Jethro:

Jethro started his first business in 2008. Since that time he has grown businesses in professions and categories including:

- Real estate

- Commercial cleaning and service
- Multiple locations of medically supervised weight loss and health programs
- Health and wellness supplement retail
- Small business consulting
- Reiki programs
- Medieval combat and weapons forging
- and Business Brokering nationwide

Through the experience of merging multiple entities and assets into one of his businesses, Jethro became immersed in the details of brokering and the unique challenges that have to be worked through to achieve success. During his initial time in real estate and learning the agency laws, he discovered that many people seek to work around or completely disregard the boundaries and expectations of their roles in the process - all in the interest of making a quick buck or actually taking that buck from someone on the other side regardless of the ethics involved. And it is this experience and valuable eye opening that motivates Jethro in how he has built each business thereafter.

In professions with rampant problems and where it's generally accepted that they mostly have bad reputations, Jethro has continually built teams and operations that defy these industry norms to bring a different level of service and expectations to his internal teams as well as his customers.

About Jeff:

Jeff Dousharm started his first business, in martial arts, in 1994 and still owns that original business. Since that time he has started or bought, and grown businesses in categories and professions including:

- Martial arts academies in multiple states
- Top martial arts and fitness franchisor in the country as recognized by Entrepreneur Magazine
- Digital marketing and lead generation
- Consulting, coaching, and masterminds
- Managed services
- Commercial real estate development and management
- Residential investment, development, and management
- Extreme obstacle racing
- Personal safety and firearms training
- Custom computer solutions
- Engineering consulting
- Marketing and sales application platforms
- and Business Brokering nationwide

Jeff is a sought after speaker and best selling author in multiple areas who brings his experience beyond his academic degrees in both engineering and organizational leadership. And though Jeff's accolades, awards, and accomplishments are meaningful in their own right, he is often respected more for what he's been through and what he's done despite these challenges. More of his personal story can be read in other books and publications, but Jeff has been told on multiple occasions that he was not expected to live.

After being a terrible micromanager in his first business, Jeff discovered that his stress, personal losses, and lifestyle was driving his health into the ground. Facing challenges with a medical condition called Ulcerative Colitis, he eventually reaches the point where cell dysplasia sets in and is turning toward cancer. And in the very abbreviated version of his life events - multiple surgeries, complications, blood clots, pulmonary embolisms, and trips to Mayo Clinic later Jeff is able to now look back at the times where his life was expected to come to an end yet he was able to make it through. This is the pivotal time in his life that changes how everything happens now in his businesses (hint: he's no longer a micromanager) and how his approach has helped and continues to help so many others.

Whether he is consulting or speaking at masterminds and conference events, with organizations and universities, or even one on one with clients, Jeff is able to take some of the most complicated issues and break them down to actionable and relatable lessons. In each case, he helps people transform their business and personal life by using the "**Lever**" to dominate the competition without giving up their time (and sometimes the competition is simply all the things we allow into our lives). The Lever is a 3 part system that involves a focus on **Time, Team and Tools**. And elements of this system are incorporated into the core of this book, **Exit Lever**, because the principles apply to many of the areas we will share with you.

Today, people often comment on how irrationally passionate our team is about helping people, just like you, to navigate the obstacles when it comes to buying and selling a business. And that is because we have seen what happens when good people have deals go bad.

This frustration drove us to do more.

We know it can be done right, and we are sick and tired of seeing people ruining deals, both as the Seller and Buyer. After all, this is one of the biggest transaction types anyone could be involved in, and you deserve to get it done RIGHT!

We are here to give you a big advantage in any deal - whether you're buying a business, selling a business, or even building your business to one day maximize the sale as part of your empire.

We're going to pull back the curtain and show you the mistakes that Sellers and Buyers make.

And by seeing these pitfalls ahead of time, you will be able to identify and avoid the issues that have tanked other deals and have devastated the value and profit from far too many transactions.

From our experience in working with others who have been burned, we assure you that there are few things worse than looking back after the transfer of a business and having a mountain of regret set in because you realize you should have done things differently.

And before someone reads this book and decides to send us a note, let's invite the elephant in the room to come out and we'll just knock him down:

Some brokers, bankers, and even business owners really don't like us.
(and we are OK with this)

And it's because we share things with you that they <u>don't want you to know</u>.

They prefer to hold all the cards when it comes to these kinds of business transactions. A more educated person sitting across the table from them is a threat to those who want to try to pull one over on you.

So we are 100% OK with not being liked, because we are sick and tired of good people getting screwed over or tripped up by avoidable problems. In fair and ethical business transactions, nobody has to get the short end of the stick! We believe in this crazy notion that each side can win without having to victimize the other parties involved.

So why are we focusing on mistakes in this book?

It's because, the big picture is straight forward or logical enough for buying and selling a business. The very simplified version is that you get a willing Buyer and a willing Seller, write up the contract, secure the financing and boom….done (kinda). But it's the mistakes that blindside people and cause all the time and money to get drained from even the best deals whether you are the Buyer or the Seller.

Some call buying and selling businesses an **art** form.

Some call it a **science**.

And while there are definitely both art and science aspects involved, the truth is that it's a big opportunity where the following reality smacks people in the face:

In buying/selling a business, one or both sides often leave money on the table and fight through endless (and needless) headaches.

This is what sours people's experiences and rightfully scares people when considering the whole ordeal. Waking up sweating at 2 AM is not the plan when people go to buy or sell a business, yet it's one of the most common experiences when "stuff" starts to hit the fan.

We've all experienced or heard stories of someone:

1. Selling their business and regretting how it went or how much they got paid for it.

2. Buying a business and feeling like they got absolutely screwed on the deal.

3. Missing the right opportunity and <u>time</u> to buy or sell.

4. And worst of all - getting tangled up in legal problems with the deal!

The good news is that it's all avoidable when you know what the hazards are and how to navigate the perils and potholes.

And when you go over the information and examples we are here to share with you, it will help make sure you aren't making the mistakes, leaving money on the table, missing opportunities, or dealing with all the headaches and legal issues. Each of the following sections are broken up into the common categories of mistakes that even smart business owners make. We're going to share examples, additional details, how to avoid the problems, and how to make sure you are getting what you need in each area!

After we share the information in each section, we are also going to have a place for you to make notes. We want this book to help dial things in for what YOU need. **And by taking notes or jotting down your takeaways you will be able to retain and use more of what you discover here!**

Remember:
6 Months and $135,000+ is on the line!

note: as you go through this book you'll also notice 3 roles that are intentionally capitalized to help identify these key positions in the deal:
Buyer, Seller, Business Broker

Mistake 1:
Don't Marry
on the First Date

Like many things in life, there is a process you can follow to get things in the RIGHT order when buying and selling a business. When you follow things step by step, it all locks into place to deliver an expected and consistent outcome. There isn't a bunch of guesswork or luck involved in good business transactions. It comes from strategy, planning, research, and executing the right system to make that happen. You don't want to just leave it up to chance when it comes to something this important.

Think back to every skill you've learned as a kid and as an adult. Whether it's how to play basketball, build a puzzle, drive a car, or bake a cake, there is a process and order to get it right.

And if you try to go through the process out of order or skip steps you end up with about as much success as asking someone to marry you on the first date.

And heck, even if they said yes, that's probably a sign of even bigger future problems.

We generally get better at any process through focused repetition and by learning from our mistakes. Once we are good at something, there is still a possibility of error; but our confidence grows through each success and we are able to navigate and continue.

So here's the challenge:
You don't have the luxury of learning from your own mistakes in buying or selling a business.

This isn't about tasting a terrible cake or grinding the gears of a car, there is a lot more on the line. It is simply too costly unless you don't mind throwing away 6 months and $135K+ for each mistake in the process.

So it's important to understand and learn from the mistakes of others. We've had multiple clients try to do it "their way" or attempt to circumvent the processes - and to date EVERY SINGLE one of them has regretted it because it cost them time and money by not following our guidance.

Learn from Bob's mistake.

We list a construction services company for sale with a considerable amount of interest. Bob, the owner, is a very agreeable Seller and easy to work with at first. He has invested decades of his life in building his empire. His business is well staffed, runs on great systems, and has many loyal customers and vendors. Selling the business is his key to retirement and the perfect way for him to cash in on what he has built, and move on to his dreams of traveling with his wife and their dog who never leaves his side.

But the deal goes sideways.

A group of prospective Buyers gets the general information, does the meet and greet, receives the financials after the non-disclosure agreement, and walks through what is needed. But instead of locking down the deal with an offer, the Buyers keep requesting more and more details about daily operations and log sheets, client lists, weekly breakdown of employee hours, and 15 years of tax returns. These are the kinds of details that should be handled after closing during the training and transition process.

So this deal gets held up in the weeds because the Buyers are doing things out of order and keep grinding out Bob's time with no real progress for over 6 months. Then, without our knowledge the Buyers go to the bank to talk about financing, and even the banker shakes his head wondering why they are meeting because there is no offer to even move on and consider financing.

The Buyers then threaten to abuse the Seller's patience and good nature by trying to contact him directly. In the end, they waste a lot of people's time by continuously ignoring the process until finally (and with our heartfelt agreement) Bob says he is done with them. And Bob, being in the construction services industry and naturally blunt, says it in a much more colorful way, but let's just say that transaction was 100% done.

This type of mistake is common, and it's better to cut ties with anyone who continually violates the process or it will

COST YOU. The Buyers in this case missed out on a fantastic deal and wasted well over 6 months of time for themselves and others. And after burning bridges with the brokers who had what they needed, they were back to square one to waste other people's time. Thankfully there was a happy ending for the Seller and we were able to get a better Buyer to the table and close the right deal. This is a great example of how you want to operate and control the process and communications during the deal. Once Bob gave us the thumbs up to kick these guys to the curb, we were relieved and got back to working with serious Buyers, which is how we ended up getting him across the finish line.

So let's get right down to it. What do the details about the process look like from a Buyer and Seller perspective? It is valuable starting this review with a look on each side.

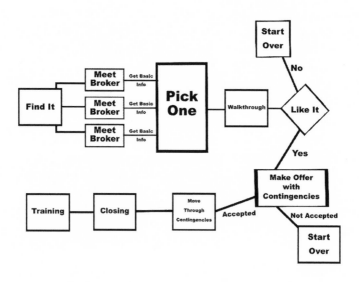

BUYER

The process is a road map. And any time you get off the prescribed roads to take, people will start randomly doing things or following the path of least resistance. And this is a sure fire way to run into problems (sometimes even legal ones).

When you map out the process but don't follow the steps in the right order that's also when you may get overwhelmed by little details. Buyers get buried in the minutia that doesn't matter. And you can waste a lot of time or end up in paralysis from over-analysis.

We had a client who was absolutely certain that they needed to hold up on an offer for a deal because they wanted access to a (confidential) list of past clients for a business. And they hadn't even made the offer yet! Thankfully we reigned them in, but for a time they were more concerned with talking about random details vs. following the process to get them where they wanted to be.

During the process, people also sometimes look for a 100% guarantee on everything.

And though we all seek out certainty in life, the reality of business is that we can't always have guarantees on everything. And when Buyers bury themselves or get stuck on things that don't have a major impact on the future of the business, they lose track of the things that actually matter far more.

Managing risk is part of any business success; and the secret is accepting that instead of being paralyzed by it.

The process follows phases. And understanding this will reduce any Buyer's anxiety.

The initial phase is a **courtesy** on the part of the Business Broker. The real work phases start once an offer is made.

And these phases start a framework, an order, and a timeline for every piece of the deal.
Examples of Phases for a Buyer:

- Find Business of Interest

- Intro with Broker & NDA

- Basic Financials/Confidential Info for Review

- Meet & Greet at the Business

- Offer Phase with Contingencies

- Due Diligence, Financing, and Release of Contingencies to Prepare for Closing

- Closing

Without this, the process can go on indefinitely and not close in a timely fashion. This can happen with an unskilled Business Broker. But more often than not, it's due to a Buyer not listening.

AND take special note of the mention of contingencies. This is a powerful tool for the Buyer to mitigate risks or concerns with the buying process. This can give peace of mind when managing the risks both known and unknown for the new prospective Buyer.

And here's the secret that many Buyer's don't understand:

You can lock down the deal
with an OFFER!

This gives you the opportunity to resolve the contingencies with deadlines, but once the offer is accepted the DEAL is YOURS and you lock out everyone else until it closes or defaults.

Here's how it works:

If there is **ANYTHING** you are concerned about in the deal, you add it in the notes of the formal offer through the broker as a contingency. These contingencies must be addressed and "released" as part of the overall process. The reason for this is to keep the deal moving **and because some information will ONLY be provided after a formal written offer is submitted.**

Often times an overanxious Buyer will be frustrated by the required order of operations due to their inexperience and even try to skip steps or try and circumvent things to satisfy their need to feel in control. And when the Buyer doesn't get what they want up front (because they aren't following the right steps) they get caught up in things that hold up the entire process. A Business Broker will then need to have very direct conversations with them on these matters. The Buyer should not take it personally, but instead realize that the broker is actually protecting their interests as well.

Here's what happens (though most Business Brokers won't tell you it this bluntly):

When a Buyer gets lost in the weeds or resists the process being communicated, the Business Broker ends up looking for others to work with because they don't want to waste time on you when they aren't getting paid.

Here's what smart Business Brokers also know - within 7-14 days of sharing the business financials with a Buyer, if the Buyer hasn't made a move, they most likely won't.

In fact, the statistics are that over 75% of deals have offers in that timeline. So showing a Business Broker you are serious is critical if you want to stay engaged in the process.

And while involved in the process and everything that goes into the ordeal as a Buyer you are best served to communicate with the Business Broker and accept very direct communication back. Brokers are better off to be direct and blunt vs. being wishy washy, and you would RATHER them be this way. You aren't involved in this for a buddy, but rather a professional you can trust to get the deal done.

Think of it this easy example. You talk to a Business Broker out of state, tell them you are interested and want to fly in for a walk through and make a written offer (which is smart to be direct about this).

BUT...the Business Broker isn't direct and isn't managing their Seller the right way, so you find out only once you land that the Seller doesn't want to walk through with you.

Again, this is why you want a broker who is direct and blunt about controlling the process so everyone involved can achieve the goal.

SELLER

So when it comes to the process on the Seller side, what are the issues?

Like the Buyer side, the Seller sometimes gets hung up on the wrong details. In this case it's on listing agreements and details that don't matter.

For example, one client got stuck on a clause in the deal that had a very small likelihood of ever occurring and the Seller didn't even fully understand the legal ramifications. This can be a good time to ask questions, but for the most part remember Business Brokers are using agreements that are designed by highly paid professionals (attorneys) who were tasked with protecting everyone involved and keeping the train on the tracks. So smart brokers will drop a client before altering their agreement in a way that creates unnecessary risk for everyone based solely on a Seller's inexperience or their feelings.

And while we are on the subject of attorneys let us be very clear on something right now:

If things end up in a legal mess or in court, the ONLY parties who win are the attorneys.
Court equals LOSE-LOSE.

You may lose time, money, emotion, and more when things go to court. So, even if you "win" you lose.

OK, back to the topic now.

The next thing Sellers get hung up on is negotiation. Perhaps some have watched too many movies or TV shows where they overdramatize negotiation tactics. But whatever the source is, we have encountered some Sellers who think it's strategic to want to argue a petty part of the deal in the 11th hour. They had the winning deal in hand, but they wanted to feel like they got one more thing over on everyone. And we have seen this cause deals to go down the drain and the Seller ends up regretting it all. This is being dime smart and dollar stupid.

Other examples include issues like when we had Sellers finalize a deal and then try and walk off with some of the TVs that were mounted in the business and included in the deal. Seriously, they just tore them off the walls! And in their mind, they got free TVs for the kids.

Winning, right??

But the reality is they almost tanked a 7 figure deal over 3 year old TVs worth maybe $100 each!
So, no. Definitely NOT winning.

Besides getting hung up on these areas how else can a Seller make mistakes in the process?

The answer to this gets to root of the importance of simply having a process.

The mistake some Sellers make is listing their business with a broker who just lists and prays.

Or worse yet, the owner lists it themselves and thinks things will happen somehow.
Either of these methods are fine for people who want to TALK about selling their business so they feel important and feed their own ego. But for those who actually want results, this is a recipe for stress and heartache.

When selling your business, the broker should have a marketing plan and process to identify the RIGHT potential Buyers and get them through the phases needed to bring the sale to a close. If they don't have this in place, or can't confidently answer your questions…RUN!

As a follow up mistake to this issue, Sellers can also drop the ball when it comes to providing the information needed for the marketing and communication processes with prospective Buyers.

Once you have listed your business, your broker should be a VIP when it comes to prioritizing your communications and follow up.

The generally accepted time frame is a 2 day window to get any info your broker needs. However, the simpler time frame of **RIGHT NOW** is better. Otherwise, prospective Buyers simply go look somewhere else where they can get what they need from Sellers who are serious.

Next up is the BIGGEST and most DANGEROUS
mistake relating to the process. This is an absolute deal
killer for Sellers. And this mistake is simply doing things
out of order.

**If the Seller gives a prospective Buyer access to
too much confidential or critical information, you
are giving them the gun to kill your company.**

The deal could fall apart and the potential Buyer could go
start their own company from scratch with the information
shared and become your competitor. You'd have to prove
they harmed your company and the burden of proof is on
you. You might get something in the end, but what usually
happens is that it takes a few years. And meanwhile, you
lose half your customers.

And what if they waited 6-9 months and start that business
with your trade secrets and confidential information?

Are you going to track them and watch what happens with
you customers?

Do you want to gamble with your business?

So when it comes to the order or things, the walk through,
and the disclosing of anything to do with your business the
Seller is best served to LISTEN to the broker and know
when to simply STOP TALKING themselves out of a sale
(and we mean this in the most respectful way).

And the final mistake we want to make you aware of for
Sellers when it comes to working with a Business Broker is

that of marketing and positioning. Unless you are an advertising professional (and even then), let your broker word and design things for marketing. Let them position your business for the walk through. Let them prompt you on what to say or not to say during the marketing process - and make sure everything goes through THEM. They are there to serve you, so make sure you let them!

So, don't ask someone to marry you on the first date - follow the process. And, in the same manner, follow the right process and steps when it comes to buying or selling a business, otherwise the Exit may not be what you planned!

Exit Lever Notes and Takeaways:

_____

_____

_____

_____

_____

_____

_____

_____

_____

_____

_____

_____

_____

_____

_____

_____

_____

Mistake 2:
Inflatable Gorillas
and a Handshake

Would you buy a used car from a random used car sales lot with big inflatable gorillas and do the deal on just a handshake with no paperwork these days?

Would you sell your house on a verbal agreement and just hope they pay?

Would you rent out a reception facility for something important based on a phone call where someone just says "yeah we'll try to keep that date open for you"?

If any of these agreements aren't in writing, you are taking pretty big risks and asking for trouble.

The same goes with just about everything relating to closing a deal on the sale of a business. It needs to be in writing. And this is true for both Sellers and Buyers!

If you aren't keeping track of things in writing such as contingencies, resolutions, and extensions (that are sometimes done verbally), the whole deal can go bad, the deposit is gone, and the Buyer walks.

Unfortunately we have worked with clients who have faced this EXACT situation. The deal fell apart because they failed to do the right things in writing.

Learn from Andy.

Years ago, we had a restaurant listed for sale with a gentleman named Andy. Andy owns a couple of businesses and the restaurant was a great asset, but he needed to focus on other goals. So he lists the business with us and we begin marketing for the right Buyers.

We very quickly bring a Buyer to the table, get an offer in writing, and the offer is accepted. From here we move on to working through the contingencies as part of the process mentioned before. One of the contingencies, of course, is getting the lease transferred. So we contact the landlord who is very agreeable since the terms would be the same and the Buyer is highly qualified.

But, we figure out that the process is going to actually take slightly longer than the original written offer and deadlines due to needing the legal teams work on the lease. So instead of 45 days it is going to take 60-75 days. This is no big deal, and we go through this process from time to time. We can simply update the paperwork and move the closing. We ask if everyone is good with it and everyone agrees. We ask the Buyer to sign off on our paperwork to amend the offer and closing. But he insists that they shook hands on the verbal agreement and that's good enough. We advise the Seller, but he goes against out advise and gives in to the verbal and handshake deal. So in the end, nobody is willing sign paperwork because they thought it was all good.

Then the reality hits. The day after the contract is supposed to close (the original deadline), the Buyer calls and demands his deposit back. And legally we have to give it to him and the deal is dead - all because nobody would sign our one page amendment. This is why we say WRITING OR NOTHING.

In the end that Buyer got caught up in other bad faith deals and eventually got put out of business through playing games with too many powers that be. Karma gets you sometimes. But in the end the deal wasted quite a bit of time and lost money for everyone involved.

After this event, which happened quite some time ago, we actually updated our closing documents and offer agreements to have more specific language with teeth for those Buyers who disregard our requirements and can make them liable - thus further protecting the Sellers and our brokers. Now we no longer have to accept a Buyer refusing to sign paperwork as we did at the time. They follow through on our process or they are on the hook.

To further underscore the fundamental importance of doing things in writing, banks can't even start the underwriting process until the offer is in writing.

We have also had a jeweler, a retail store, a medical related business, and several service based businesses all contact their banks ahead of time and each of them were confused when they couldn't move forward (despite our very specific instructions in the matter).

When it comes to banks, without the written offer…

They can't start the appraisal.

They can't check credit.

They can't do an approval.

Why? Because banking and financial business is done in writing through very specific documentation and processes.

So when it comes to getting things in writing, you also have to be sure you are getting it done properly.

If your attorney is not a business attorney, or if your agent is a real estate agent who doesn't do business specifically (even if they do commercial real estate), then they likely don't have the right paperwork for the processes you need!

Moreover, they also don't know how to value things properly because it's not their normal operations or type of business. This becomes even more critical outside of the handful of largest metropolitan areas in the United States as they would have even less access to accurate or comparable sales in the given market. This is the difference between someone who can stumble through the process vs. someone who does it for a living.

Exit Lever Tip for Buyers & Sellers:
Ask any broker or agent to SHOW you, in writing, the comparable sales they are using to value your business. You

wouldn't list your house without comparable sales so why would you do this for your business?

One of the common mistakes we have also faced from clients related to this issue is relying on email for an offer. Some turn to email because this is a social norm. But...

Email is not considered an offer in writing and not binding because anyone could have used that email account.

And just having it in writing is not enough for a legally binding offer, the format matters as well. There are elements of the offer that matter for spelling out the right details to protect ALL the parties. Clients may not see all the issues to begin with, and that's all the more reason to work with professionals who can protect you all along the way.

Another mistake relating to doing things in writing is more of a Buyer dominant issue from our experience. And this is having their attorney write up an offer from scratch instead of recommending changes to existing broker documents. By making changes to existing documents and tools provided by the broker or advising attorneys, the Buyer can save both time and money.

Standard procedure is for ALL parties to use the same documents from the Business Broker that can be reviewed by attorneys of all parties.

We have had Buyer attorneys start the documents from scratch. That means the Seller attorneys then have to review and clear them or recommend any changes. And then our (the broker) attorneys have to do the same. This process becomes circular as any and all comments or changes require all three sets of attorneys to then pass things back and forth and continue to run up the bills while twisting the clauses meant to protect everyone.

Business Brokers have an obligation to both the Buyer and Seller to protect the process of the deal. They are legally liable as part of it all, so trusting and following them is an important way to protect yourself.

Additional Exit Lever tips when it comes to doing things in writing:

1. If you are a Buyer, putting in writing what your key points are or what you need will help make things VERY clear to the Business Broker. This will ensure you get better results and accelerate the process. Writing puts a framework on things and allows for better work to be done.

2. Sometimes a Seller talks to a Buyer without the Business Broker. And then the broker has no idea what was said, promised, presented, agreed, and yet the broker is on the hook and should have known what's going on. This quickly spins into a nightmare for everyone involved. So keep it in writing and through the broker!

So let's avoid doing deals on shady car lots with inflatable gorillas and hoping a handshake deal is going to protect us. And let's make sure EVERYTHING is in writing whether you are the

Seller working to Exit the business or the Buyer looking to take things over!

Exit Lever Notes and Takeaways:

_____

_____

_____

_____

_____

_____

_____

_____

_____

_____

_____

_____

_____

_____

_____

_____

_____

_____

Mistake 3:
Is the Water Hot or Cold?

We have a bucket of water and ask you to put your hand it it.

Is it hot or cold?

Odd question that you can't really answer, right?

Let's make it easier by adding some context.
We have 3 buckets of water in a line in front of you going left to right.

The one on the left is very hot.
The one on the right is very cold.
The one we asked about originally is in the middle, and that bucket is a temp half way between the two other buckets.

So we ask you to stick your left hand in the left bucket which you can barely stand due to the heat.

We also ask you to stick your right hand in the right bucket, which is equally as shockingly cold.

And after complying with our requests we ask you to take both hands and put them in the middle bucket.

As you can imagine and feel right now…
Your left hand coming from the hot bucket feels COLD in the middle bucket.

Your right hand coming from the ice cold bucket feels HOT in the middle bucket.

This is because the middle bucket has a sensation or feeling that's relative to the comparable temps of the other buckets.

You may have heard or even seen this example before, and it's all the more relevant to business sales when it comes to evaluation what a business is worth.

A business has value RELATIVE to multiple factors and one of these factors is COMPARABLE sales.

So a business by itself is difficult to know what it is really worth, just like when we asked you if a bucket is hot or cold before having other buckets for comparison.

We have run into this time and time again, and though we had two specific examples we'd like to share, our attorneys advised us not to because some of the details we would need to share to make it relevant would be in a gray area of breaching confidentiality, and we just can't do that no matter how juicy the story is - because we respect others too much.

So the summary of two stories you would have read summarize to:

1) A franchisor convincing a franchisee that their business was worth far less than it really was, and

2) A group of Business Brokers convincing a business owner that their business was worth far more than it really was in order to get the listing with their company due to the owner being excited about the higher (and unsupported) valuation.

Both situations caused a great deal of anguish and problems for over a year for the respective owners.

But in each case, once the business owners came to us, we were able to help them alleviate their frustrations and show them better ways to do it right and get them to their goals.

Unfortunately, some business owners and Business Brokers don't get the right value on the business for a number of reasons.

Some of these reasons for getting it wrong include:

1. They rely on a generic multiplier instead of drilling down to more specifics for the right kind of business.

2. The Seller or the Business Broker doesn't have the experience or skills to put together adjusted financials for the appropriate add backs in the valuation process to get to a more relevant value.

3. There is sometimes confusion by Sellers and even some Business Brokers on the differences and when to use

Gross Sales, EBITDA (Earnings Before Interest, Taxes, Depreciation, and Amortization), and Seller's Discretionary Earnings in calculating the value of the business.

4. And the dirty secret that some Business Brokers try to gloss over is that they don't have access to the right databases for comparable sales. And this is a critical step in the valuation process if you want to get it right.

Sellers working on their valuations without getting this list right are going to really struggle. And for Business Brokers who get it wrong - it's unethical and unforgivable in our opinion.

Our position on this may be another reason why some Business Brokers and realtors don't like us, but here's the truth:

Too many Business Brokers and realtors are operating in a way that they cannot possibly perform the due diligence to best serve their clients.

They try to cut costs and find short cuts so they don't have to invest too much time, but in reality they cut out a major portion of their duty to their clients. This is sometimes the case when a residential realtor or new broker with little or no additional experience and training attempts to put together a business deal where they are outside of their scope of competence. Doing a deal once in a while doesn't replace the experience, tools, and special skill sets need to best serve clients when it comes to business transactions for both Sellers and Buyers.

Without doing a valuation with some basis on comparable sales, Business Brokers are NOT getting the right value determination for you!

So why don't some Business Brokers do this?
The simple answer is that they don't invest the time or resources to acquire the education and/or tools to evaluate the businesses they are supposed to be serving. You may have heard some brokers or owners even say casually dismissive things like they just valued a business based on a "Rule of Thumb".

But guess what? Rule of Thumb doesn't hold up in court. Having a real valuation method is defendable to banks, courts and more. And shocking to some, is the fact that the market value of the business is sometimes not even what the CPA says it is.

Listening to friends is also not a reliable valuation process. And, of course, having your emotions overly invested in a business doesn't mean it's worth more either. We have had many owners who love their business (as they should) and because of that love they have an inflated sense of what their business is worth. Though well meaning, it's simply not justifiable or marketable if they are serious about selling.

Finally, on some occasions, the value of the business can even deviate from what the market appraisal says!
Blending multiple methods for valuations and then weighting the ones most relevant are how you get to the right price.

Doing it the right way you will have an asset valuation, a future earnings valuation, and a market valuation. And ONLY when you put these factors together in the right way can you say that you have a good valuation.

There are also instances where we have had a bidding war in the market for a specific type of business and it even exceeded what a bank will lend on it despite market pressures or bidding. And that's where cash can be brought in on top of the SBA financing to keep the deal on the table and going even higher! Again this is where having the right professionals involved makes all the difference for our clients.

On this note we want to clarify a position about realtors. You will find several comments and notes regarding realtors throughout this book. So let us be direct about this so there isn't any confusion or misunderstanding, we don't hate realtors. We love the great ones. And we know that the bad ones who show poor professional judgment hurt the rest of their industry and ours.

As referenced earlier, when a realtor (or anyone) operates outside their scope of expertise and in areas where they don't have the experience or tools necessary, their clients suffer because of it. So if we love the good realtors, what does that mean and what's the difference in this context?

The sharpest realtors we have ever met make an intentional decision in the area of brokering businesses to do one of two things:

1) Develop a relationship with great Business Brokers where they can still participate and profit in the deal as a

referral source when they have clients who need to buy or sell a business.

2) Invest the time, training, and effort to gain the skills and consistently engage as a real Business Broker in addition to being a realtor. There are some who do this and add a great division of services to their business when they do it the right way.

On the other hand, the realtors (and even part time Business Brokers) who don't put in the investment to develop and maintain their skills and experience are doing a real disservice to their clients. And every time they operate beyond their professional scope and capabilities they are rolling the dice with disastrous risk for themselves and the people they are working with.

Exit Lever BONUS Tip:

The other mistake people make related to the valuation and financing process is getting an appraisal done at the wrong time.

Most often this is well meaning, but violates what we talked about in the previous chapter about following the process. The prime example is when we have seen the Seller get the appraisal done ahead of time (against our advisement). And then the Seller is frustrated because the bank can't use that appraisal! The reason for this is because it's not neutral if the Buyer or Seller orders it.

**The exception to this is if there is speciality equipment that needs to be appraised to even generate a valuation to begin with in the listing process.

So remember: the **bank** needs to order the appraisal or that water from the bucket we talked about in the beginning is definitely going to feel bad when reality sets in!

Ultimately your ability to sell or buy a business RIGHT relies on getting an accurate and supported valuation of the business.

Part of this process MUST include multiple valuation methods and finding out the value by comparing relevant sales in the market, just like comparing the temps of the water buckets we mentioned at the beginning of this chapter!

Exit Lever Notes and Takeaways:

_____

_____

_____

_____

_____

_____

_____

_____

_____

_____

_____

_____

_____

_____

_____

_____

_____

_____

Mistake 4:
Missing the Toolbox

Imagine if you roll into a car mechanic shop with your luxury dream car and just need some basic maintenance. And while you are getting checked in you look into the shop area and notice that the only tools the mechanics have in their toolboxes are hammers. You would be concerned about having your car serviced there, and rightfully so!

The same is true when we look at a business whether you are a Buyer or a Seller.

The business needs to have the right tools in their toolbox to operate as a real business. And in this case, those TOOLS are SYSTEMS. Without the right systems to operate, the Seller's business value is diminished, and the Buyer's chances of success are slim. Part of what is being sold in the whole deal is the Toolbox or systems to make everything work. So if some of the tools or the whole toolbox is missing - you've got problems.

This is also a key component for those planning ahead or starting a business so you can scale and maximize future value!

When someone goes to sell their business, having systems makes all the difference in the valuation because if the business relies on one owner too much then it's not really a business; it's a job. And it's a lot harder to sell a job than a business!

Meet Dr. Allen. We met him during a conference that a group of our brokers and owner/consultants were taking part in as advisors. In this conference, many dentists were looking at ways to expand, protect their assets, and transition to more investments for passive income. There are many great strategies and people involved in this process, and we want to focus on one particular facet of Dr. Allen's example. You see, Dr. Allen's practice was very successful, but it had one major issue that he hadn't considered. He was a solo practitioner with his wife as the practice manager and had been trying to sell the practice to no avail.

Though dental practices can be very valuable, the few who looked at his practice asked simply:

Why would I buy your practice when they all look at you as THEIR dentist - and when you leave, they could just as easily jump to another practice in town vs. accepting me as their new dentist? And on top of this your wife isn't staying and you have no business systems or automation in place to help things continue to run!

This is not always the case, but it was a harsh reality that was staring him in the face where he realized his practice was far too dependent on him and his wife and what they knew in their heads vs. what was operating independently of them. It was not a turn key operation at all where someone else could take over and many figured out that they would be better off just opening up as his competitor instead if they wanted to get going in that market.

So at the conference we walked him through a two part strategy that would help him prepare the practice for sale. First he brought on an associate who would transition with the practice in addition to giving them options for partnership. Second, we had them document the systems. Dr. Allen was very stressed about this and we realized he wasn't the detail oriented person when it came to the systems. He was an amazing clinical dentist but he enjoyed helping the patients, not running the business itself.

However, his wife was a world class manager. She just didn't have things documented because she relied on her own skills to run a tight ship. So all this really took was having her carry around an iPhone with her to either video or talk her way through each thing she was doing. This was then transcribed and edited to turn into their operations manual. With this in hand, less than a year later, their practice sold for a greater value and with very little problem in the transition.

Now do dental offices sometimes sell from a solo practitioner? Of course they do. But they do not carry the same value, and it's easy to show that another dentist could just open up their practice instead of overpaying for patients who are about to be abandoned by "their dentist" as he or she retires or moves on.

So what if you aren't a dentist?
The example is even more relevant as many businesses rely far too much on one key person - the owner. And when

this is the case there is not as much value in the business itself as a sellable asset.

So what does this mean to you? As a Seller, as much as possible, your business should be documented through SYSTEMS on how to run it all vs. just being in someone's head (owner or otherwise). And when looking at a business as the Buyer, you should be looking for this key factor as well - and use it as a negotiating piece on overall value.

The simple logic is this:

The more your business works without you, the easier it is to sell.

The more critical you are, the less the business is usually worth because there are more Buyers and investors looking for passive income, or turn key businesses than there are people looking to buy themselves a set of chains to tie themselves down to the business with no freedom or flexibility.

That said, there's also a difference between being there and HAVING to be there.

We all know that some owners are involved in the business because they simply love being there. If a business owner is there when they WANT to be, and the operations can run without them, then it's still in a very good space and has options for future owners to do the same on their own terms.

So what about those looking to build and position their business for the future?

Document the systems and automate as much as possible. The less YOU do, the more it's worth! Automation doesn't always mean technology and robots or anything. It just means YOU don't have to make it happen or serve as some kind of bottle neck for the processes.

Another metric to consider is this:

If you can't train someone in 28 days to be able to do what you do (90% or better), then you have a problem.

There are a few exceptions that have more technical needs, but most businesses are about handing off the reigns properly to make a smooth transition. And if this takes more than 28 days, the business likely has too many internal problems and needs clarity.

So when we work with clients looking to prepare their business for sale, we recommend to review and see if there may be opportunities to make improvements to maximize their position. And when looking to buy, you can focus on this area as a way to compare opportunities!

Part of the value of what is being sold with the business includes the TOOLS or systems that are in place (or needing work). So be sure to ask the right questions to be sure it's not missing in your business!

Exit Lever Notes and Takeaways:

_____

_____

_____

_____

_____

_____

_____

_____

_____

_____

_____

_____

_____

_____

_____

_____

_____

_____

Mistake 5:
Getting Run Over

Will Rogers has a great quote that goes:

Even if you're on the right track, you'll get run over if you just sit there!

In business the same holds true. If we sit too long, eventually we will get run over. There are peak times to sell or buy a business.

Here's a simple rule - if you HAVE to sell, you waited too long! You missed the best window of opportunity.

We had a business listed for sale for Rob, where he had been gradually downsizing year after year. He and his wife were ready to pull back and focus more on enjoying their lives. They had built a comfortable lifestyle they could maintain and it was time to throttle back on a few of their business endeavors. So as part of this he started making changes but he just wouldn't let go of one of his businesses completely. They owned a transportation and entertainment business and he had been taking a couple vehicles out of service each year to make things easier, but still wasn't ready to sell it all off. What that really results in is steady margins but a sinking gross income year after year. It wasn't because he couldn't get the business or was doing anything bad. It was because he was intentionally tightening things up and scaling back.

So when he did finally get super motivated to sell, the lender looked at the business going from twelve vehicles to four, the declining revenues, and a 25% year over year overall decrease and questioned the sustainability of the business venture. This means they the need to look even harder at the Buyer to be stronger as it's considered a higher risk venture. Since he waiting too long in the process, Rob and his wife ended up sacrificing a great deal of value in the sale of the company. If he had just sold it all earlier when they started cutting back, he would have gotten a premium on a booming business. Instead he had to settle for a fraction of what could have been, all because of bad timing and decisions for the long term vision.

Besides the example above of timing combined with decisions that could adversely impact you, there is also the factor of rushed timing. If you HAVE to get out in 3 months, 6 months, or some type of fast exit, then you waited too long and you definitely won't get a top price. And you may not even be able to sell at all because everything happens in certain timelines. And if you try to compensate by discounting the business too far it scares away the market (except for people who you don't want anyway).

If you are desperate to sell, then Buyers can take advantage of your situation. This is a sad situation we have seen too many times and is one of the risks of long term business ownership without the right strategic plans or exit strategies.

So what kinds of things could happen to cause this?

Here are another few personal and simple questions:

What if you die?

Is your business partner or partners in a position to carry on or sell the business without you?

Is your spouse in a position to deal with them or sell properly?

If you are vulnerable to a situation where you could be pressed to sell your business fast, then we advise you to create contingency plans now — or you could be putting the people you love the most in a terrible position where they have to deal with not only the emotions of the situation at hand, but also the torture of then having to pick up the pieces of a business that is unraveling.

And this can be as easy as creating a folder with the proper advisors that contains a list of instructions and directives for carrying out the contingency plans to make things easy.

Now let's take that a step further. Maybe it's not death. What if you get severely ill, injured, or incapacitated in some way?

No matter what, having the plans in place ahead of time will provide peace of mind for when life happens.

Here's another statistic involving 6 months that should make you think:

In the event that the primary operator dies or is in anyway removed from the equation in running a Main Street business, the business will shut it's doors forever in an average of 180 days!

Besides avoiding the urgent sale, timing is also about the dynamics of the sale for each phase. For example banks take <u>at least</u> 2 months just for their phase of financing. And if a Buyer delays in getting all of their information in, it screws up the timing even more.

So what are some things owners can keep in mind to avoid this kind of tragic position or missing the right window of opportunity when it comes to timing?

The most fundamental thing is that you don't want to sell at the absolute peak or after the peak of your business, but rather on the way up. This may sound counterintuitive to some owners who think the goal is to sell at the absolute peak. But selling it on the way up helps ensure the Buyer has a good year too! As the Seller, if you carry part of the financing, this makes sure you get paid!

More often than not, we have seen Sellers miss the peak itself and sell after the peak - yet still think it was worth what it was at the top. If you peak and then tax returns go down, you now have negative trending and look like a business that needs to be "fixed". Those businesses sell for less because they look like a sinking rock. And often this is compounded by an owner who is becoming burned out.

Finally for those who think you could just dump your business, and then it's all on the Buyer to deal with any problems, know and heed this **WARNING**:

*If the SBA provides financing on the
deal and the business then goes under
in first year, everyone is getting sued...
and it's by the government...so the
odds are not in your favor!*

**If you want to have the best results and not get
run over by sitting on the tracks too long, exit
your business with the right timing.**

**And on the flip side, if you are a Buyer, look at
more than just the current financials to
determine what the timing is telling you about
the real and expected value of buying that
business. Sometimes the timing can give you an
incredible deal, we just have to be aware of any
associated risks!**

Exit Lever Notes and Takeaways:

_____

_____

_____

_____

_____

_____

_____

_____

_____

_____

_____

_____

_____

_____

_____

_____

_____

_____

Mistake 6:
Don't Be Blockbuster

Once upon a time there was a company called Blockbuster. You may or may not even remember all the details, but we all know they were the dominating industry leader when it came to movie rentals.

Then through a series of bad strategic decisions they ended up getting destroyed. Some say it was market disruption, but it really wasn't. They had plenty of opportunities to control the emerging markets when it came to subscription services and even streaming media.

Instead they made short term decisions that led to long term disaster. Hindsight is 20/20 here, of course, and they didn't see the writing on the wall at the time.

We can take this cautionary tale and apply it to strategies to multiple areas. In this case we want to talk about it with a focus on taxes, financing, and tax structured legal entities. When you get these areas wrong, you are risking going the way of Blockbuster.

First up, to get this note out of the way:

If you are selling a C-corp, it creates additional issues and tax consequences.

A selling entity that is a C-corporation, will pay federal and state income taxes on the net taxable gain from the asset sale. If the corporation then wants to distribute the proceeds to its shareholders, each shareholder will then also be taxed on the amount distributed to him or her.

But if you work with the right people ahead of time (3-5 years for example), there are steps that can be taken to save money. So a little bit of time can be your friend when planning out your tax strategies and exit plan.

So besides C-corp issues, what else should you be aware of or mistakes should you avoid when buying or selling a business?

As a Seller, understand that when your Business Broker tells you that you should owner finance part of it, it's not just about making an easier sale. There are tax benefits to owner financing part or all of the sale.

On top of this there are tax and legal aspects of using funding sources such as a retirement account to buy a business. In this case, if a Buyer doesn't document the investment properly and communicate with their tax professional, the Buyer could face some major consequences on their taxes.

Again note: we are not CPAs and we are not dispensing financial advice here other than recommending that you speak with your CPA and Business Broker at the right time to review how owner financing could benefit you.

Next up, and one of the most common issues we run into with certain categories of business is that of overly-aggressive tax strategies. We recognize and appreciate saving taxes, but when done at the wrong time we have had clients use those "tax saving tactics" that saved a dollar for them that year but cost them 4x that or more on the sale of their business! So don't fall into this trap yourself.

SDE, or Seller's Discretionary Earnings, is one of the top metrics for determining the value of the business.

And this ends up being a multiple in the valuation of the business when it's time to sell. What that really means is that every mistake you make here costs you many times over in the valuation.

So, **at least** the year before you disclose, showing and paying taxes on everything may help maximize your business value. Consider this: you may pay 30 cents on the dollar in taxes vs a 3-5 times multiplier on the valuation and sale.

So let's say you hid $100,000 worth of profits and saved somewhere around $30,000 or so in taxes depending on your specific situation. You pat yourself on the back for getting one over on the IRS (it's illegal, but you somehow assure yourself that you are keeping more of what's yours and it's a victimless crime or something along those lines).

And then because you are selling your business that same $100,000 worth of profit would have increased the value of the business by $400,000 if your industry multiplier justified a 4X value on the SDE or EBITDA.

So now you saved $30,000 in taxes and lost $400,000 in the sale. And it could be even worse!

That math makes it easy to see short term vs. long term planning and how it can impact your financials.

So plan ahead for what you want more of, and of course speak with your CPA on these matters.

As mentioned, there are certain categories where tax issues are more common. And if you also run a predominantly cash business like a bar, liquor store, or other cash businesses you need a Business Broker who can explain and market how the business is run. Creativity in how your business is run is fine, but you as the Seller better be able to have the right ways to show **provable** methods to help the Buyer see how it all works. And your word isn't enough.

If the business for sale needs a bank loan, the Seller will have to show documentation and proof of financials. And the less a Seller can do this, the tougher time the Buyer will have in getting the loan approved. So it's in everyone's best interests to get this done right in a manner that a reasonable banker can follow the paper trail to validate the numbers and values being stated.

We have had multiple clients run into this position and there are ways to come up with good solutions and acceptable methods. The key is planning ahead and being proactive vs. just being reactive when the bank or the Buyer starts poking holes in the deal and challenging the authenticity of the numbers being presented regarding the value of the business entity.

In the end, the more cash business you keep off the books the more you will either have to owner finance the deal or the less you will have to take for the company.

The hard rule is: You can only use what you can prove when valuing a business or applying for a loan.

And so if you don't want to go the way of Blockbuster thanks in part to bad decision making, then don't use bad tax strategies when selling or buying a business!

Exit Lever Notes and Takeaways:

_____

_____

_____

_____

_____

_____

_____

_____

_____

_____

_____

_____

_____

_____

_____

_____

_____

Mistake 7:
Pulling The Carpet Out

Sometimes the carpet is clean but it's pulled out from under you!

One of our clients on the Buyer side, we'll call Dale. Dale is a great guy and has the experience and skills to make a great acquisition with one of several of our listings. After reviewing several great options, he chooses to pursue a highly successful carpet cleaning company that we recently listed. After the walk through, reviewing the financials, and considering each area of the long term opportunity, Dale makes an offer. With a little bit of back and forth of countering and contingencies, the owner accepts and we start talking about banks and lenders.

Dale decides he is going to go with the bank where he has been doing business. It's a fairly large national bank, so there shouldn't be any major issues in approving a loan of this size. And then we start interacting with the lender to drive the process forward and it becomes apparent that something is out of place. Even though he is a commercial lender, he has clearly never done an acquisition loan.

So the lender hands off the loan to a local SBA agent, who works on it for about a month before handing it off to a regional SBA agent in Colorado. The regional SBA agent then works on it for another month before kicking it out to the big processing center in California.

We usually tell our clients that if it goes to California, they no longer want to get the deal done and they are just looking for reasons to say no.

> *NOTE: this is not a claim as to the SBA or the performance of any particular lender, but rather our view on the experience from many transactions.*

So during this process the lender:

- "misplaces documents" more than once

- refuses to communicate with the Business Brokers

- refuses to accept documents from the Business Brokers

- forces the Buyer to become the middle man with the Business Brokers

- has both Buyer and Seller redo financial profiles as they move the loan to a new SBA agent

- and finally tops it all off by convincing the Buyer to **massively over collateralize the loan**

We advise the Buyer to talk to another lender, but the Buyer decides to stay the course despite the circumstances. So now we have a deal where the Buyer has put his acreage, his other business, a 20% down payment and an owner carry of

20% all on the line with an agent who, in our opinion, has done a disservice to the Buyer in the overall package.

At this point we get a phone call from the bank. We are holding the deposits in company escrow, so they assume we are the title company as well, and order us to do a title search on Dale's acreage in another state. We recommend several title companies they could work with as it would be inappropriate (and outside our capabilities) to provide these services.

They move forward, and five months after the Buyer signed the offer we get a call from a title company. The bank has now told them they are going to do the closing on this sale in 5 days. The title company has no documents, no idea whats going on, and needs us to send them the escrow deposits and details on whatever we need.

Just two days before closing, the title company decides they have satisfied the deposit verifications, and will now be using all of our brokerage documents since the bank has sent them nothing.

Then on closing day the real nightmare begins…

All the parties are sitting at closing.

All NCBA documents are present and in order.

All NCBA managed deposits are accounted for.

BUT, the bank has not provided any required documents for the closing.

Finally, four hours after the scheduled start time, the bank documents arrive. Frustrated by the delay, but glad to be done everyone signs, shakes hands, etc.

And then the question arises:

Where's the money?

After signing, the title company informs us that the bank has not funded the escrow account for closing.

This means:

1. The Seller has not been paid for his company.

2. The broker has not been paid the commission.

3. And the Buyer has not been provided the operating capital that is a part of the loan.

As a bonus, this also qualifies as a massive case of fraud as all documents state money has changed hands.

So everything has transferred including utilities, lease, payroll, billing, titles, and all that goes into the transaction itself. Yet, the money is missing.

We spend the next two weeks doing everything we can to remedy the bank's breach of performance. And, of course, everyone is talking to attorneys due to the issues at hand.

The bank cuts checks to the Seller and the broker at about the 3 week mark after closing.

Then the bank cuts the operating capital check to the Buyer at around the 6 week mark after closing.

At 17 weeks after closing the business is approaching bankruptcy, and selling off assets.

And at 28 weeks after closing the business declares bankruptcy.

Without the operating capital that was required, there was no smooth transition of operations. Dale did not have the liquidity to keep everything running, nor should he have been expected to by the letter of the contracts. By the time he got the capital from the bank it was too late to save him; he had lost employees and his accounts.

In the midst of the dumpster fire that had formed through this process, and around the 30 week mark, the SBA sues every party involved except the bank.

Dale loses everything including both businesses and his acreage.

The Seller loses the owner carry and court costs in the process of proving he didn't sell a lemon.

We as the broker lose massive court costs in **proving** the bank was actually the only guilty party in the transaction.

So, in the end, everyone took major financial damage. The difference is that except for the bank, it was due to no fault of their own.

Business sales transactions are a great wealth building process for both the Buyer and the Seller when it goes right. And this example underscores the importance of working with the RIGHT lender vs. just settling for a bank who means well or getting passed around to agents who clearly don't have the competence or integrity to do what's right.

It only takes one bad lending agent to pull the carpet out from underneath this or any other business.

So this takes us to the next logical issue. Some might suggest that you avoid the SBA entirely because of this example. And that is NOT at all the point we are making here. The reality is that **over 90% of Main Street business transactions end up being an SBA loan**. The key is working with the right kind of SBA lender and the right SBA loan program.

There are several types of loans, and the SBA can help determine what the best one is.

So if we know the SBA (Small Business Administration) is going to be involved, how is there a mistake to avoid?

The mistake is going to the wrong lender.

You don't want to go to some random bank, your buddy, or even your regular bank.

Our clients have had much greater success through a relationship and working with an SBA PREFERRED LENDER.

What that means to you as the borrower is that these lenders do enough volume and deals that they can more easily cut through some of the red tape. This process is already long enough and complicated enough as it is, so it's better to have a powerhouse in your corner to help things go your way. And the right Business Brokers should have relationships to help you.

And, if your SBA Preferred Lender can work with a regional SBA office vs. working with the national office, you will usually have an even better experience and improved time frames.

SBA loans take on average 45-90 days. And they could take up to 2-3x that long.

The less you have followed the structure and order of the deal, then longer it's going to take at this point. Your Business Broker should already know at least 75% of what the SBA will need right off the bat. They needed this information to value your company if they did it right.

Once you are in the SBA phase of the process you already have an official written offer.

WARNING FOR SELLERS:

Many think the SBA process is all about the Buyer, but it's not. Sellers, in this phase if a Business Broker tells you to get something, you better jump because when the SBA wants something you need to not drop the ball with them….or else you won't end up getting a check!

Here's another fact that few people know, and that many brokers don't want to tell you:

More than half of deals fall apart after the offer is accepted, so this isn't the time to back off and celebrate!

You don't want to spend 4 months going through the SBA process and have the deal fall apart. So view it as more of a pass or fail FAST scenario - so if it fails, you can get it back on the market for another Buyer if you need to!

Another step that great Business Brokers can help with is regarding problems with the banks. One of the steps in the solution to this is to get a deal **SBA Pre-Qualified**.

This means an SBA Preferred Lender has taken the time to review the assets, inventory, financials, and history of a business that a Business Broker has listed for sale and says this business is a lendable enterprise and makes enough money (cash flow) to meet the SBA guidelines. SBA Pre-Qualification can save time when it comes the lending process and create even more value and validation for an interested Buyer.

And in the end, if you can't get a loan approved on it, <u>it is the Buyer's fault!</u> It means they are not liquid enough, don't have the right experience, or they have an issue with their creditworthiness.

And on the flip side, for a Buyer, the SBA Pre-Qualification saves them a significant amount of time. By working on a deal with this already in place, they can avoid the games and stress caused by many lenders.

And as a reminder, though some may want to work with a "local bank" or "their bank", it isn't usually worth the tradeoff of time, money, and headaches that come with a less experienced or less accredited lender who simply don't have the same tools as an SBA Preferred Lender.

So if you don't want the carpet pulled out from underneath you, the right banks and lending options are critical to getting the deal done!

Exit Lever Notes and Takeaways:

_____

_____

_____

_____

_____

_____

_____

_____

_____

_____

_____

_____

_____

_____

_____

_____

_____

Mistake 8:
Banks Don't
Let Paint Peel

One of the things we've always noticed about every bank we work with is that they are NICE.

Have you ever looked around many banks?

Marble floors, or extremely nice carpets, immaculate fixtures, and fresh painted walls are par for the course when you enter a bank. There is no paint peeling off the walls. There are no holes in the floor and no shag carpet from the 70s. Part of this is to assure you of their stature, security, prominence and everything else that goes into the experience of banking at their institution. And part of it is, frankly, because they can afford it.

We can all agree that banks make really good money. And we aren't vilifying them for this. As the phrase goes, "if you can't beat 'em, join 'em." Pretty much everyone has had some sort of frustrating experience or a time when a bank gave them a hard way to go. And in the end, we can either stay mad or we can take the lesson and do something with it. And one of those lesson is to consider the options, in full or part, of playing the bank yourself.

Sellers and Buyers often overlook cash options and what it can mean for them in arranging the transfer of a business.

A route that some go is to incrementally sell portions of the business. This carries a bit higher risk since the Seller will still be tied into the business with the Buyer. However, this can work very well in some situations depending on the goals, timelines etc.

Another option is to owner finance the deal.
Let's face it, banks make loans to make money (and they make a lot of it). And a business owner selling a business has the same opportunity and tools that the banks do. Unfortunately, it is an option many choose to ignore, and in doing so rob themselves of a valuable revenue stream. So, we advise Sellers to at least keep this option on the table and consider the pros and cons involved.

In the case of owner financing, it is usually wise to get a chunk of the money as a down payment. And, of course, in this scenario you can repo the business if things do go bad. But also realize there is likely going to be big drop in it's value and position if that happens. So with this in mind, Sellers also have a vested interest in setting the business up to do well under the new Buyer.

In owner financing situations, smart Sellers should get a personal guarantee which then may let you go after other assets the Buyer owns if their is a default. Getting that guarantee requires the negotiation and agreement done right to protect you. Again this is where the wrong kind of agent or even an owner can drop the ball and wind up not getting you the money you deserve.

As mentioned in a previous chapter, owner financing may have some benefits for a seller. For example, CPAs have shown Sellers how owner financing gives you the benefit of spreading capital gains out over multiple years. This may help you from jumping tax brackets, offset with other expenses, and even other tax benefits that your CPA can advise you on. Many owners have found that by owner financing larger chunks of their business, they end up appreciating these additional upsides they had not considered when first looking at selling.

Sellers sometimes look at it as a more risky proposition. But let's look at the reality of the net gain:

Playing the bank allows you an additional revenue stream with compound interest - often at at a slightly higher rate.

Sarah, who owns a fantastic service based company with a good team, is looking to step into another business to continue to grow her empire, and she knows it is the right time to sell. After listing with us, we run several direct marketing campaigns and locate an ideal Buyer for the business, Anthony.

Anthony has good financials, and a strong background in the same type of services. He also has two young kids and a wife. So he is motivated to do things right and grow the business for their future as a family.
Both the Buyer and Seller are positioned to make this deal a success. Because this is a service based business, the banks

have some extra issues with the loan process. The value of the business is easily validated, but there are still hoops to jump through in the process. Both Sarah and Anthony are becoming frustrated.

Solving problems for both Sellers and Buyers is what a great brokerage can do. So, after meeting with our Business Broker team, we show Sarah there is another option she can consider: be the bank. Initially, she is hesitant as she has never done something like that before and asks a lot of smart questions on the process itself and how she can control any risks involved. Then we run the numbers for her...

- Her business has an agreed upon sale price of $825,000.

- A 20% downpayment of $165,000 leaves an 80% remainder to finance - or $660,000.

- With $660,000 financed we lay it out as just 5 years at 7% interest.

- As the Seller, she now makes an extra $167,000 in interest!

So now instead of just getting an $825,000 pay day, she would get almost a MILLION dollars!

**As always we advise Sarah and anyone to consult their attorney and CPA as to advice on how to best handle the final details and spreading the tax hit over the years for even more benefit.

Sarah is almost in tears when she sees that she can make that much more money and it's not going to take too long of a period. The proposal is made to Anthony who jumps on the deal and is happy to accept the terms.

You may be thinking, "but what if it defaults?" This is good to consider and evaluate, and the result further underscores why this can be a great process. Even if, as a Seller, you have to take the business back after a couple years, you may still have the equipment and assets to sell off and still come up ahead or better than when you sold it!

So, in any specific situation, you have to examine the options; and then be like the bank and hold on to titles of assets. Banks do this for a reason, and you as the Seller have a legal right to do it too! And if you are on the Buyer side of this kind of deal, it puts you in a place where you can make deals happen more easily and have a continued relationship with the Seller who has a vested interest in your success.

Banks don't let the paint peel because they make the extra return on their cash to be extremely profitable, and you can too.

So what we are telling you is that <u>sometimes</u> it's good to be the bank by looking at cash options!

Exit Lever Notes and Takeaways:

_____

_____

_____

_____

_____

_____

_____

_____

_____

_____

_____

_____

_____

_____

_____

_____

Mistake 9:
I Know Everything

For both Sellers and Buyers, ego sometimes gets in the way.

For Buyers it usually has to do with being realistic and practical about what it's going to require to run that new business. Money isn't always enough. Certain skills and mindsets have to be in place.

If looking to buy a business, it should be something you have real interest in and have some background or skills that match that business. This may sound like common sense, but it has to be said because we have seen it disregarded too many times.

Besides general interest and listening to the Business Broker, if you are looking at a business that has employees, then having experience with employees matters. And if you don't have a specific needed experience or skill set, then you need someone on your team who does or you are lowering your chances of success in the long run.

Pretty much anything can be learned, but the better of a fit a Buyer is for a business, the lower the overall risk becomes.

Good Business Brokers also guide Buyers to the right business match. Otherwise they are on the hook to explain to the judge or the SBA how you put together a deal like this and allowed it to blow up. The broker is there to do more than just sell the business. They are there to protect and increase the chances of success for everyone.

On more than one occasion we have had to tell prospective Buyers, "DO NOT BUY THIS BUSINESS" because we have an obligation to make the deal NOT implode.

Part of ensuring this process and the stability of any deal is the fact that Sellers need to fully disclose everything about the business. The law is funny about this. Even if you don't know, but you could have or should have known as a reasonable person might - then a Seller is presumed to be as guilty if something goes wrong just as if they willfully concealed something. So a Seller needs to understand that by not telling the Business Broker something important they are not making it easier to sell the business, they are just adding legal risk. So it's better to be transparent with your broker.

Once the Seller is transparent about every area of the business with their broker, then it's up to them to continue to uphold their due diligence in working with prospective Buyers. And this is where the previous point comes into play about saying now. Just because a Buyer has the money to buy a business, and thinks they can run it does not all ways mean they should pull the trigger.

When a broker does this, they risk tens of thousands of dollars in commission. It doesn't mean it's a bad business, just that it is a bad business for you. And when a good broker does this, they maintain their integrity in the best service of both the Buyer AND the Seller because when deals go bad later it's not a WIN for anyone.

For example, a Buyer named Jonathan is very excited about a $360K deal. It is a deal put together for an incredible price as the business could go for over half a million, but the Seller is very motivated for other reasons and prices it to move faster. As we move through the process, it becomes apparent that the long term potential in this deal is a bad fit for the Jonathan because he simply lacks the time required to commit to the ongoing operations. In this case the business is one that needs the Buyer to be a true owner operator and be on site in its daily operations. So we advise Jonathan that this really isn't a good fit and that we can help him keep looking for something else.

Before we go on, let us underscore the reality here - advising Jonathan to pump the brakes means we are putting a $36,000 commission back on the shelf and even rolling the dice a bit for finding another future Buyer. But it's 100% the right thing to do as our integrity is not for sale to make a commission by doing the wrong thing.

Now back to Jonathan. He is not happy with our advisement. In fact, he ignores our advice to walk away. He explains very eloquently that he is a smart guy, that **he knows everything** about business, and that this business is different (this is always like nails on a chalkboard when we hear this one).

On top of our conflict with Jonathan, our Seller is also fairly upset with us because he just wants the deal to be done no matter what, even if there is risk of consequences later (which is a very risky position to take). Despite our professional position, the Seller also insists on ignoring us and moving forward with the deal.

As a result, a solid business that's been around over twenty years gets sold.

The Buyer is happy!

The Seller is happy!

And then the reason for our advisement, based on our experience and insight, comes to fruition…

In the coming year the business goes bankrupt as Jonathan attempts to be an absentee owner. Even though he thought he knew everything and that his business would somehow be different, this smart guy rides the business into the ground like the Titanic getting raked on the iceberg.

On the way down, the Seller loses $60K of owner carry in the deal.

Jonathan loses $300K invested in the business.

In the end, everyone loses: Jonathan, the Seller, the customers and more.

We didn't need to tell them that we told them so. We actually hoped that he would make it work somehow. But as we have all seen, hope is not a solid strategy for real success when it comes to business.

So here's the lesson:

If a broker who only gets paid when the business sells, tells you this is not the right business for you and that you should not buy it, you should immediately come to a full stop and think for a bit. Otherwise you may be running right at the edge of a cliff.

In addition to this kind of scenario, there are a few other issues. On the Seller side, ego comes into play and can be dangerous too. It usually results in NOT listening to professionals such as their Business Broker, and this is how they get in over their head. Sellers don't need to just get creative, they need to ask for advice. The broker is there to advise. And if you don't ask, some brokers may not think to bring things up that could help you.

Finally for Sellers, a big and beneficial skill is knowing when to stop. During communications with a prospective Buyer, we have had Sellers allow their ego to prompt them to keep bragging and puking all over the prospective Buyer to make sure they know every single thing that comes to mind. And though it is sometimes well intended, the result is that it may overwhelm the Buyer.

On top of talking too much, Sellers may even say something the Buyer ends up perceiving as a big negative - like something or someone the Seller ends up complaining about. Some Sellers start talking to a prospective Buyer like their buddy and next thing you know they are venting about whatever is on their mind and their current frustrations. And in those kinds of conversations they start needlessly shooting holes in the value of their own business!

So let us remind you now: Sellers need to know when to stop talking.

Saying less is often better vs. talking yourself out of the sale.

This is not to imply that you would or should mislead anyone or not disclose essential information. But you don't need to get a Buyer lost in the weeds or completely confused early in the process.

You have plenty of time to review and assist in the transition after closing.

So let your experienced Business Broker take the lead here and follow their direction when it comes to laying out all of the information needed in the right time and place. This is similar to previous issues we brought up with regard to the process. But in this case it's more a matter of sitting back a bit, and allowing the right things to be said at the right time like all of the instruments coming in on the right times in the orchestra.

So when it comes to selling or buying a business, instead of thinking that you know everything in the process, check your ego at the door and listen to the guidance and experience of trusted professionals who are on your side!

Exit Lever Notes and Takeaways:

_____

_____

_____

_____

_____

_____

_____

_____

_____

_____

_____

_____

_____

_____

_____

_____

_____

Mistake 10:
Wakeup Call

Early in the book we mentioned how some people wake up at 2 AM sweating and how this isn't what most people plan or hope for.

Yet here are a couple of statistics that shock many people:

1. **Only 25% of businesses listed for sale, ever actually sell!**
2. **Only 10% of business owners use a Business Broker.**

Now let's take a look at the first statistic a bit deeper:

75% of businesses listed NEVER sell!

What that really means is that 3 out of 4 businesses listed for sale after years of hard work, sweat, sacrifice and surviving all of the pitfalls get to the stage where they should cash in- and it simple doesn't happen. Imagine a family business closing because it can't sell to someone else to take it into the future. Or imagine a company with a team and staff who care, yet feel like they are now riding the Titanic in a business that was ready for new ownership, but couldn't make it happen. Both of these and many other scenarios happen and it's heart breaking because it doesn't have to be like that.

So what about the 10% statistic? If 90% of businesses are selling without a Business Broker then that sounds like the thing to do. Go with the masses, right? Except that you are probably already wise enough to know that the masses are seldom right. This also helps explain why the masses never end up selling their business successfully. Would you rather be in the top 10% or bottom 90%? One is a bigger group, but bigger isn't always better.

We almost made this mistake category and discussion the first one in the list of ten we are sharing with you. It is the most important one. And as you can see with a statistic like 90%, it's often the most violated and common mistake we observe.

We also know that if we jumped right to this issue, it would fall upon deaf ears for many who would only believe it once they experienced the catastrophe themselves.

We have been sharing real experiences and a behind the scenes look with each example and mistake up until now. And no matter how you buy or sell a business, this information can absolutely help you. So, by now this sharing should have built a certain amount of rapport and understanding between us to the point you're ready to read one of the most important truths you'll ever see in selling or buying a business:

If you try to do it all yourself when it comes to selling or buying a business, you're setting yourself up for failure.

We don't advise people to do their own legal work, their own taxes, or their own dental work. So why on earth would you get involved in something as important as selling or buying a business on your own? This isn't like running a garage sale, this is about significant financial and legal matters. So you should control the process by assembling the right TEAM to make it happen.

This is not a self-serving position. It is an experienced and blunt warning. If you are selling or buying a business, you are getting in the ring with others who don't represent your best interests, and may even make mistakes. No matter what, you want to maximize your opportunities whether you are the Seller or the Buyer.

Here are some things to consider if you think of avoiding Business Brokers so you can supposedly "save":

Do you want people walking in off the street and talking to your employees, chatting with your customers, or even interrupting you during business hours to ask about details or money? Or would you rather focus on your business? How critical is it that your vendors, employees and customers NOT know your business is for sale? Wouldn't it be of value to keep things confidential so you don't risk any of these relationships until it's the right time to control the communication and transition?

How did you value the business and validate it if you are doing it on your own? Is it defendable in court?

How much time do you have in a day to run two jobs? Because when you list yourself, not only are you trying to run your business, but now you are also in charge of marketing it, selling it, dealing with banks, solving contingencies for closing, and hoping not to miss deadlines.

When you do this you aren't saving time or money like some convince themselves when making a bad choice. In fact, you are losing BOTH time and money.

On average a good Business Broker will help you earn, save or retain at least TWICE their broker commission. And in our opinion, doubling up on ROI is good no matter what the deal is.

And besides the commission side of things, what happens when things go wrong?

Who is on the hook legally and financially?

How do you protect yourself and those counting on you?

Now, you may be dismissing this and telling yourself, "these guys are saying this because they just want me to list with them." So let us continue to be very BLUNT with you (and we do this out of actually caring):

We aren't worried about listing your business.

If you are reading this book, there's only a small chance of us taking the next steps together…..and that's ok!!

We aren't desperate for listings, and we turn down plenty. So nobody on our team of Business Brokers is ever going to put a hard sell on you or we would terminate their relationship with NCBA.

Our lifestyle and our company's financials aren't hinging on a desperate attempt at getting you as a client. That said, you may have the potential to be a GREAT client. And if there's a way we can help you with our Business Brokerage, consulting, lenders, or any other business relationships we have - then we are here for you if you're a good fit for our team.
But we didn't write this book to beg for clients. We published this book to HELP YOU, and we published this book to SERVE...because we are tired of good people getting bad deals in the process of selling or buying a business.

So, now that we have that out of the way, let's go back to the good stuff and how you can avoid other mistakes.

The other mistake to avoid in this category besides not using a Business Broker is continuing to treat the broker(s) involved in the deal as the enemy.

Yes, the Business Broker works for the person paying them (generally the Seller). But their job is to get EVERYONE across the finish line.

So if you will listen to the broker, even if they aren't yours - will get you to know what you need.

A good and ethical Business Broker does not want to set up either party for failure. Keeping this in mind then, treating the broker as a neutral party gets you a long way. And the broker can serve you as a great free asset.

Business Brokers cannot harm their client, but they can recommend additional relationships or resources, due diligence to be done, and help you in the process itself. In nearly every case, the broker only gets paid when they get the deal done....so they are there to help.

What if as a Buyer, I want a Business Broker to help me find the right business deal to purchase?

This is a smart move that Buyers can make to get a pro in their corner to begin with if they aren't already connecting with one through a listing. Good Business Brokers can serve as a Buyer Broker. And the process is very similar in finding out what you need, and how to find a business that best matches your goals and long term vision.

The difference here is in how the broker gets paid.

Some brokers will offer their services "free of charge" as a Buyer Broker. And here's what we've found when this happens - you get what you pay for. Those who offer the service free and tell you they just get paid on the sale from the Seller are telling part of the truth. The "rest of the story" as Paul Harvey would say, is that they have no vested interest to find you a deal vs. any other Buyer. You will not likely get as much action or service as you hope and you will be <u>frustrated</u> by the slow progress.

So more experienced or valuable brokers require a deposit up front to represent a Buyer and go hunting for the right business for them. But don't worry, this is mainly to filter out the tire kickers and people who want to talk about owning a business vs. really taking action. At closing, the Business Broker **should** credit or factor in the deposits or fees to the final commissions.

By handling it this way, the brokers are motivated to do the work. Otherwise, they face situations where they may never be compensated for their hours and efforts because the Buyer never pulls the trigger.

Robert is a great example. He is looking to purchase a landscaping company after working for multiple other employers and saving up what he needs for a downpayment. His goal is to buy one versus opening one because he has seen too many other startups struggle for too long and he would rather have the stability of starting with accounts, clients, and great positioning right from the beginning of ownership.

In order to represent him and go find the best fit, he puts down a non-refundable deposit of $1,000. And it is agreed that each time we find him a deal and he does not buy, he puts down another non-refundable fee of $1,000.

In the process, we show Robert three landscaping companies that fit the parameters of what he is looking for. So the total fees paid in are $3,000. And after the third company walk through, Robert makes an offer and deposit, and it's accepted! At closing, the Seller pays out our commission and the $3,000 is then reconciled with the Buyer as part of the closing itself.

But what if we never closed on the deal and Robert kept changing his mind?

This is exactly why the fees are in place. It ensures that we work with serious Buyers.

Robert was very serious and so he had no problem with this process. He valued our time and knew that he would do better with us than on his own.

Basically, anyone who refuses the small up front investment or deposit shows us that they are not serious and will just be wasting our time. This is the best litmus test so we don't end up wasting time when we could be working for Sellers and Buyers who actually want to make deals happen.

Exit Lever BONUS Tip:
In this section we also have to mention the sad drama that goes on between way too many Business Brokers. And this is revolving around broker splitting.

Weak Business Brokers don't broker split because they are greedy and short sighted!
*calling them out on yet another issue may not make us popular with some brokers…but we are here to tell you the truth even if they don't like it!

You can see their greed in the fact that they want to ONLY take the whole deal vs. splitting with another broker. In other words, they will only do the deal if they are the only broker involved so they don't have to share or work with anyone else. These are the same brokers who will sometimes try to force a deal in hours instead of giving things their proper time and place in the process.

Meanwhile, a 60/40 split (Seller Broker/Buyer Broker) is smart and puts the client's goals first.

But some Business Brokers would rather have the business sit and not sell vs. doing what's right for the clients and getting the deal DONE!

And the few brokers who do broker split, often don't work with local Business Brokers because they figure local Buyers will eventually find them anyway.
So instead of fostering trust with their clients, driving more deals to close, and building long-term relationships that would serve THEM and future clients, these Business Brokers would rather camp out on listings and pat themselves on the back for only doing deals to get 100% of the commission.

Here's our perspective - nothing of any real significance has been done by just one person. We rely on a team in our Business Brokerage including our internal people, vendor relationships, and even other outside Business Brokers (the few who broker split) because we know this is what leads to the WIN for everyone.

Does it mean we give up some commissions?

Yep.

And we more than make up for it in the long run by doing what's right for our clients.

We own our businesses and know the kind of integrity we would expect - so we provide that and more for our people, and YOU should look for and demand this level of service with any Business Broker you work with!

This being our last mistake to cover before going on to the valuable Bonus Section, we sincerely want you to avoid that 2 AM wakeup where you are sweating, shaking, or filled with worry and regret. And the right way to do that is working with the RIGHT Business Brokers and not treating them like the enemy.

Exit Lever Notes and Takeaways:

_____

_____

_____

_____

_____

_____

_____

_____

_____

_____

_____

_____

_____

_____

_____

_____

_____

_____

Bonus Section: Picking the RIGHT Business Broker

We've brought you this far, sharing the 10 Mistake categories where you now know how to navigate and avoid problems.

So the natural question most intelligent Sellers and Buyers have is:

How do I find the RIGHT Business Broker to help me?

There are plenty of Business Brokers out there, <u>both good and bad</u>.

And in developing our company we looked for key differences that make the greatest impact. First and foremost we are business owners ourselves, and so we know what matters to owners - both as a Buyer and a Seller. And we built our policies and processes to SERVE our clients and make the experience better.

The following list will help you see how we are different from most and let you know **what to look for in a broker (and why)**.

1. Certification

In some realms of business, certifications and credentials matter, and in some they don't. With something as important as buying or selling a business, it's important to know that there is some level of accreditation, accountability and certification involved. Anyone on the street can call themselves a Business Broker, but what does that really mean?

Are they a member of any professional organization?

Do they have any real training or affiliation with educational programs?

Are they just a realtor who tries to do a business deal once in a blue moon?

We recommend working with Business Brokers who are IBBA certified. We **require** all of ours at No Coast Business Advisors to be IBBA certified so our clients can have peace of mind knowing our brokers are prepared to best serve their interests.

What to look for:
National Certification & Credentials

Biggest benefit for you:
Greater assurance that the people you are trusting are qualified.

2. REAL Business Experience

Your experience as an owner simply can't be replaced by theory or books. As mentioned in the very beginning, we own multiple businesses outside of brokering. We have decades of experience and the background to bring valuable insights to the table that can only come from having paid your dues. What this means to you is that you are working with people who are just like you - not someone who has never sat in your seat or known the challenges you face.

There's a difference in this kind of relationship so we recommend that you work with Business Brokers who have been through the complex situations and trials that come with being an owner.

What to look for:
Business Brokers who have owned or had solid business experience outside of brokering

Biggest benefit for you:
They speak your language and more fully understand your position

3. Network of Business Brokers Nationwide

Why work with just one broker when you could work with a network to find more opportunities?

We have multiple locations and Business Brokers. Working with a network of brokers means that you have more access to deals as both a Buyer and a Seller.

So, whenever you evaluate a broker to decide the best fit for your needs, ask about this kind of access. Do they bring an expanded reach and networking muscle from being a part of a larger entity, or if they just play small on their own.

What to look for:
National network or team

Biggest benefit for you:
Greater connection on deals for Buyers and Sellers

4. Local AND National Markets:

In addition to having multiple brokers in a network, operating in both local and national markets means that great Business Brokers are going to work and reach out through multiple geographic areas to connect the right deals.

When you are limited to just a local market for prospective deals, you may miss out on opportunities.

And on the flip side it's also important to have boots on the ground and the right relationships in the local markets to provide the best service for clients.

By operating in both local and national markets the right Business Brokers will get you the best of both worlds.

What to look for:

Business Brokers who operate in both local and national markets

Biggest benefit for you:

Access to more opportunities to connect the best Buyer and Seller for a deal

5. Advanced Valuation Tools & Software

As we mentioned in an earlier chapter, how a Business Broker values a business is critical to your success.

So when you meet with or evaluate a broker, be very direct in asking how they value a business.

If they don't have the tools and software to produce the best valuations, then you are setting yourself up for additional problems when it comes to financing, closing, and maybe even leaving money on the table.

At NCBA we use a blending of three accepted valuation methods including comparable sales. This helps our clients get the valuations they need to deals they deserve.

What to look for:
Business Brokers who can show you multiple valuation methods provided through advanced tools and comparable sales

Biggest benefit for you:
Better valuations eliminate road blocks to getting the deal done

6. Pre-qualified Client Listings with SBA

Having SBA pre-qualified listings means that the Business Broker has a relationship with an SBA Preferred Lender. This is a valuable resource and demonstrates the kind of investments they are putting into their deals.

When Business Brokers go through the additional work to process and get deals pre-qualified it is a good sign of their commitment to giving clients the attention they deserve. Not every listing can be SBA pre-qualified, and good Business Brokers know when to make it happen.

And that's why we've invested years into the right relationships to offer this service at NCBA for our clients.

What to look for:
SBA pre-qualified listings by the Business Broker you are considering

Biggest benefit for you:
Greater assurance of commitment and attention to client needs in financing and beyond

7. Active Marketing

There is a big difference between placing a listing on boards and doing active marketing for a listing.

There are some "discount" Business Brokerages, and realtors who try to do Business Brokering on the side. They offer cut rates AND of course very bare bones service provisions. And this is why so many of their clients end up leaving out of frustration and a lack of results.

When you want better and faster results, look for Business Brokers that have systemized and active marketing campaigns for their listings. And if a Business Broker can't explain to you how they do more than just throw a listing on a board, *that's a clue*! It means they aren't likely doing anything else.

At NCBA we can break down the strategies and marketing for every client and listing we have, because we know what it takes to get results.

What to look for:
Marketing campaigns beyond board listings

Biggest benefit for you:
Increasing your probability of closing on a deal

8. Support Staff & Network of Vendors

When you need something, your Business Broker should have the answers and options- NOT send you looking for them.

If you go to a nice resort or hotel and need dry cleaning done, they don't stare at you blankly and say, "well, good luck." They step up to coordinate everything that needs to happen to make your life easier.

The same or better should be expected of a great Business Broker. If this is what they do, then they should have the relationships to step in because they know what clients might need.

At NCBA, we have invested a great deal of time, travel, and resources to have a stable of great relationships, staff, and vendors to serve our clients.

This doesn't mean we require clients to use our options, but we have the resources at our fingertips to offer solutions to our clients when needed!

What to look for:
Business Brokers with business vendors and relationships to serve you

Biggest benefit for you:
Less headaches and risk searching for solutions

9. Development and Education

It's important to look at what any serious Business Broker is doing for ongoing education and development.

Every high level professional and regulated service profession has some standard or requirement for continuing education.

Unfortunately many Business Brokers only look at this as an expense, and they try to avoid it. Long term this hurts their ability to properly serve their clients.

Our team invests over six figures a year in development, education, and training. What that means for our clients is that we have Business Brokers who are better equipped to serve and deliver the results expected. Markets and challenges are always changing, and that means our team has to be lifelong learners if we are to best serve our people.

What to look for:
Proof of Business Brokers who continue to train and invest in their skills

Biggest benefit for you:
Current skills and training means they aren't operating on outdated standards from a decade ago

10. Best Selling Authors

Authors get a lot of respect.
And best selling authors get even more.

Some say, "anyone can write a book." Yet, very few ever do, and only a tiny fraction of those become best sellers.

Why is this?

The amount of work it takes to become an authority or expert in any field is challenging. And then consolidating that authority or expertise in a book that can communicate their ideas is even more difficult. And finally, putting that book and themselves out there for public scrutiny is very intimidating to most people.

And that's exactly why you would want to work with the very few who have been through it successfully: it demonstrates their authority, commitment, and ability to serve others. It speaks volumes to their power to make things happen for you as their client.

What to look for:
Best Selling Book

Biggest benefit for you:
Sign of their authority, commitment, and ability to make things happen for you

Exit Lever BONUS Tip: Work with Owners, Not Just Employees

With some Business Brokers, you would end up working with random assistants and employees. But you are better off working with an owner.

At NCBA, in addition to brokers having outside business experience, they are also OWNERS in the brokerage itself.

This means they own their business or a piece of the business as a partner. And that's a different sense of security and relationship for clients knowing that they are working with someone with a lot more skin in the game.

So, when you evaluate a Business Broker, do some digging. Find out who you are really dealing with and decide what level you'd like to work with to get the best results that you deserve!

What to look for:
Business Broker who is an owner or partner, not just an employee

Biggest benefit for you:
Working with someone with more skin in the game

Exit Lever Notes and Takeaways:

_____

_____

_____

_____

_____

_____

_____

_____

_____

_____

_____

_____

_____

_____

_____

_____

_____

_____

Want access to additional FREE resources for buying or selling a business?

Simply go to:

www.ExitLeverBonus.com

Want more information on No Coast Business Advisors?

Have more questions?

Then go to:

www.NoCoastBusinessAdvisors.com

Interested in becoming a Business Broker yourself?

Check out:
www.NCBAbroker.com

Special Offers
for our Readers!

1) Considering the sale of your business now or in the future?

Visit:
www.NCBAvaluation.com
And enter promo code "500" to claim $500 OFF your Business Valuation!
(fees applied at closing if you work with NCBA)

2) Know someone who may be interested in selling (or buying) a business?

Send them to:
www.NCBAfriend.com
They can also save $500
AND
When they fill in your name as the referral source, we'll GLADLY give you a **10% referral fee** on our brokerage commissions earned!